The
IVY
LEAGUE
COOKBOOK

The IVY LEAGUE COOKBOOK

Ruth King & Anita Hart

New Century Publishers, Inc.

Printing Code
11   12   13   14   15   16

Library of Congress Cataloging in Publication Data

King, Ruth, 1936–
    The Ivy League cookbook.

    1. Cookery.   2. Cookery—Ancedotes, facetiae,
satire, etc.   I. Hart, Anita, 1934–   .   II. Title.
TX652.K464   1982   641.5   82-14507
ISBN 0-8329-0145-8

Contents

PRIME CHART

ONE CUT ABOVE THE REST

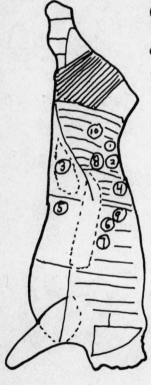

1. CHAPIN SCHOOL (100 EAST END)

2. NIGHTINGALE-BAMFORD (20 E. 92nd st.)

3. TRINITY School (139 W. 91st st.)

4. BREARLEY (610 E. 83rd st.)

5. Collegiate (241 W. 72nd st.)

6. Buckley School (113 E. 73rd st.)

7. BROWNING (52 E 62nd st.)

8. The Spence School (22 E 91st st.)

9. Miss Hewitt's (45 E 75th st)

10. St. BERNARD'S (4 E. 98th st.)

11. Miss porter's House

MANHATTAN TENDERLOIN DISTRICTS

BOSTON BEEF

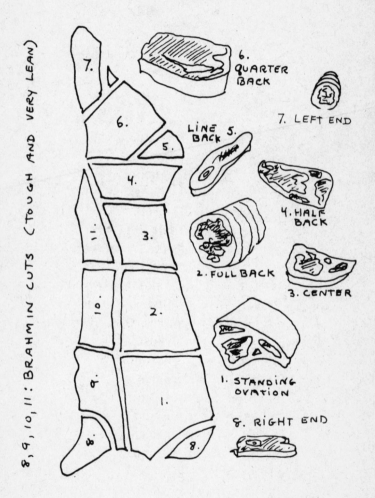

8, 9, 10, 11: BRAHMIN CUTS (TOUGH AND VERY LEAN)

6. QUARTER BACK

7. LEFT END

LINE BACK 5.

4. HALF BACK

2. FULL BACK

3. CENTER

1. STANDING OVATION

8. RIGHT END

Preface

It's cook's night out, the club is closed, it's too late to get a reservation in any really Ivy League restaurant, and anyway, the charge card needs a little rest. What to do? Ivy Leaguers never panic. Their approach to food—preparation as well as ingestion—is just like their approach to everything they do. They show the same gay abandon they demonstrate in driving, dressing, studying, and general living. And, like most things they try, their meals turn out just right—for Ivy Leaguers, that is. Taste matters, but style matters more, and spirits matter most of all.

This book is a no-sweat approach to cooking—in other words, "a piece of cake." Recipes which require mincing, dicing, many pots, watching, and general fussing have been omitted. And you don't need a kitchen that is designed by a culinary wizard with a flair for nouvelle cuisine and high technology. Even a closet kitchen will do. You can also scratch most of the utensils that turn Craig Claiborne and Pierre Franey on.

Forget garlic presses. The clove is just as

effective in powdered form or in jarred minced pieces. Who wants to get close with hands that smell? A flour sifter is positively archaic. A wok is for nerds. In fact, part of the fun will be improvising. For example, instead of a strainer you can use an old squash racquet. If a finer mesh is required, how about using a well-laundered Lacoste shirt? Measuring cups and spoons are for conchs. None of our recipes calls for exact measuring. Save that for mixing perfect drinks.

Make sure you don't buy too much. Everything should double for use in preparing cocktails and punches. In the way of electric implements we suggest only a food processor. Buy sturdy pots in about four sizes, one medium-size frying pan, long-handled forks and spoons (two each), a paring knife, two cutting knives, pot holders and dishcloths (Madras naturally), and many disposable baking pans in a good selection of sizes.

Ivy Leaguers who live at home may find that the cook has all of the above and then some, but those that have to buy cookware really do not need anything else.

The same is true of larders. Keep a good supply, but not for a famine. Have canned goodies—tuna, broth, peas, asparagi, mushrooms, water chestnuts, liverwurst, and baked beans, to name more than enough. A few boxes of assorted farinaceous products (spaghetti, linguini, etc.), minute rice, bread crumbs, dehydrated soups, and crackers can't spoil. Teriyaki sauce, mustard, tabasco, olives, bitters, Worcestershire sauce, drinks, and proper mixers and chasers will do for bottled sundries. For specific menus, shop on an ad lib basis.

Remember the freezer. Alongside of the vodka you can store veggies, spiked ice cubes, sherbets in a rainbow of colors, bread, and stocks (another name for broths). These will be your frozen assets.

Oh, and another thing. Do not get a spice shelf with a dozen useless bottles. Garlic powder, salt, pepper, onion powder, oregano, and rosemary will suffice. Remember, cuisine-wise, Ivy Leaguers are not people for all seasons.

MOBY DUCK

SAVORING
"THE JOY OF MIDDLESEX"

Cookbook Classics

There are thousands of cookbooks around. Some have even been made into fine movies by the French avant garde. They are not for Ivy Leaguers. Within the first recipes they use arcane instructions such as peel, core, clarify, blanche, and the like. We feel the following books are the only ones that we can wholeheartedly recommend for browsing.

1. Crazy Salad
2. A Movable Feast (the picnic book)
3. Moby Duck
4. A Separate Piece (an encyclopedia of finger food)
5. 100 Years of Solitary Cooking (cooking for one)
6. Under Skimmed Milkwood (for dieting Ivy Leaguers)
7. Joyce Carol Oats (the breakfast cereal book)
8. The World According to Carp (catching and cooking fish)

9. The Grapes of Roth (a guide to wines)
10. Clockwork Orangeade (speedy cooking)
11. Good-bye Mr. Potato Chips (edibles to serve with drinks)
12. Catch Her in the Rye (the bread book)
13. The Prime Cut of Ms. Jean Brodie (selecting and cooking meat)
14. Slaughterhouse Five (lists companies that are humane)
15. The Decline of Western Cooking (3 volumes)
16. Rabbit is Rich (guide to fattening foods)
17. Roots (potatoes, yams, carrots, etc.)
18. The Joy of Middlesex

Just remember, you can get all the above or none. The only book you'll really need is this one—for intimate dining for two, to asphyxiating crushes for 200.

Gruel

Before we get on with skills and technique, we have to point out that it is bad form to say "yuck" when something is presented at the table. But, it is equally yucky to serve food that Ivy Leaguers simply cannot eat—no matter how intense the drinks. We like to call these unpalatable items "gruel." The following are definitely "gruelsome."

Avoid:

Gizzards
Hominy grits
Okra
Frozen fruits
Prunes (not for regular guys)
Pimentos
Creamed herring
Gefilte fish
Sauerbraten
Poi-poi
Fava beans
Cuchifritos
Tripe

3

Maraschino cherries
Squid
Eel
Rutabaga
Lox
Polish bigos stew
Ham hocks
Endangered species

Introduction
to Menus

Well, it's time for the nitty gritty (recipe on page 67). The following are suggested menus for all sorts of good-natured occasions—engagements, graduations, reinstatement of driving licenses, end of exams, etc. All menus are preceded with store-bought appetizers such as tinned liverwurst served in a college mug, ready-made quiches, dips, peanuts, potato chips, crackers and cheeses. Naturally, cocktails start all parties.

You can end them all with store-bought desserts, although we list a few suggestions for easy homemade types. Jello, puddings, popsicles, and another round of drinks and cordials are a fun way of telling your guests you enjoy their company.

By the way, always leave a good variety of liquors and mixes visible during dinner. And, with the exception of wines which can be served in jugs, always be familiar with the Christian names of all liquors. The generic won't do at all.

It has to be Jack Daniels, Glenlivet, Chivas Regal, Canadian Club, Dewar's, Wolfschmidt, etc.

The same with fruits, which you should not hesitate to buy bruised. It proves ripeness as well as klutzy handling and, after all, what are Ivy Leaguers if not secure? Some fruit names to remember are Bartlett, Ryber, Freestone, Cling, Bosc, Comice, Delicious, Granny Smith, MacIntosh, Harvey, Malcolm, and Kerby.

Some recipes will bear an asterisk. Those are highly recommended ones which have been tried and tested in our laboratory kitchen under the strict supervision of federal agents of the G & S (Gluttony and Satiety) Department of the National Right to Food Bureau. The others sound like they could be fun, and they are guaranteed to meet the daily nutritional requirements of black mice. Good luck!

As Simple as ABC

McB. Eltee, Jr. is coming over with his wife ZeZe, his daughter DeeDee and his son Jay-Jay. Now, McB. is a graduate of U.Va. and has an MBA from U.P . He is a member of the N.Y.A.C. and the S.E.C. It's true that rumors on the Q.T. have it that life has taken a downturn for the Eltees. His son is on L.S.D. and his daughter had a D. and C., and McB. keeps dipping into his C.D. because of a wad of I.O.U.s brought about by an I.R.S. audit. However, his connections are still A-one, so mind your P.s and Q.s and treat him like a V.I.P. Suggested for this evening are the following:

Appetizers

Alphabet noodle soup with saltine crackers

FRESH KILT CHICKEN

Main Course

Chicken Little Breast*
Boiled Rice with Peas
Spinach Salad

Dessert

S & W canned peaches sprinkled with B & D

Chicken Little Breast

Five chicken breasts skinned and boned	Butter
	Oregano
Garlic powder	White wine

Have the butcher bone, skin, and pound the fresh-killed chicken breasts flat. (Don't forget to call him Sir.) Melt about ½ stick of lightly salted butter until it sizzles. Brown the chicken breasts on both sides, sprinkle with garlic and oregano, and douse with wine. Cook about ½ hour or so. (Time for 2½ martinis.)

Boiled Rice with Peas

Serve chicken on a bed of rice prepared according to the instructions on the box. When rice is ready, toss in a can of peas and mix until it is white, green, white, green, and so on.

Spinach Salad

For the salad, wash and drain, and remove tough stems from spinach leaves. It is optional to throw in bacon bits, sliced mushrooms or croutons. Sprinkle with dressing made from equal parts mayonnaise and wine vinegar. See page 67 for hints on perfect mayonnaise.

Dessert

For dessert, do not, repeat, *do not,* drain the peaches. Add plenty of liqueur and offer your guests another round of drinks.

Cooking Needs No License, But Isn't It Nice When...

Your driver's license has been re-instated. What an occasion for a special dinner! After the last scrape with the law you thought your goose was really cooked. Well, it's all just a bad scene that's over, so let's celebrate with something special tonight. How about...

Main Course

> Vest of Goose Down Home Style*
> Low Mainline Noodles*
> Lettuce with Cucumbers and Apples

Dessert
Bermuda Shortcake

VEST OF GOOSE DOWN HOME STYLE

Vest of Goose Down Home Style

1 7–8 lb. Goose Butter
Salt and pepper

Rub the goose, inside and out, with butter, salt and pepper. Cover the breast and drumsticks with a "vest" of aluminum foil. Roast at 375° for about four hours. Smoking and sizzling can be avoided if you place the goose on a rack above a pan with about ½ inch of water on the bottom. Keep adding water. After 1 hour remove the vest. Goose need not be watched too often, but remember to prick it every now and again to let the fat run out. Discard drippings and gizzards. Insofar as cooking is concerned, for some hormonal reasons, you must buy the male. Apparently what's good for the goose is not good for the gander.

Low Mainline Noodles

1 8 oz. box of thin
noodles
½ cup minute rice
1 can chicken broth
1 envelope
dehydrated onion
soup

1 canful water
1 can sliced
mushrooms *or*
1 can water chestnuts

Melt butter in a pan and brown noodles until they turn orange. Then, add all the other ingredients and simmer for about ½ hour. (Time for 2 Bloodys.) *Note*: This dish can be served with anything, but it is best with poultry where it has the same consistency as stuffing.

Salad

2 apples sliced into
    cubes
2 cucumbers peeled

Iceberg lettuce cut
into bite-size
pieces

Toss all the ingredients with dressing. See page 67 for "perfect salad dressing."

Bermuda Shortcake

Pound Cake
    (frozen or shelf)
Strawberries
    (fresh please)

Cointreau (plenty)
Sugar

Slice the pound cake about ½ inch thick. Core and slice the berries (about 3 per person). Splash Cointreau and a bit of sugar liberally. Serve the berries over the cake.

Spoonerisms

Ivy Leaguers are born with a silver teaspoon in their mouth. But, they are diffident, and because of this, they avoid the word teaspoon. Here are at least a dozen words to use instead of teaspoon.

1. A splash
2. A dash
3. A sprinkle
4. A soupçon
5. A shake
6. A jigger
7. A dollop
8. An intsy bitsy
9. A smidgen
10. A hint
11. A tad
12. A drop
13. A wee bit
14. A dab
15. A squirt
16. A touch
17. A teensy bit
18. A whisper

COURT BOUILLON

Luring, Baiting and Hooking

There is a supercute, intensely charming, lawyer who just graduated from Columbia. Want to lure and hook this intense Ivy Leaguer? Think fish. You almost said "gruel." Not so. When it's the following recipe, "one man's fish is definitely another man's poisson." Plan it this way.

Appetizers

Heavenly dip with taco chips. See page 67 for "heavenly dip."

Main Course

Gray Flannel Sole*
Dill–mayo sauce for fish*
Button Down Collards
Court Bouillon

Dessert

Columbia Law Tort

Gray Flannel Sole

2 filleted gray sole
    slices
Butter
Salt and pepper
Bread crumbs
    (seasoned)

½ small jar of
    mayonnaise
1 small bunch of dill
Juice of one lemon,
    or a good splash
    of concentrate

Season the fish with salt and pepper and sprinkle with bread crumbs. Bake at 400° for about 20 minutes. (*Time*: 2 G and Ts.) A few minutes before serving place large dabs of butter on top and allow to melt. Serve with dill–mayo sauce.

Heat and serve boiled canned potatoes on the side.

Dill–Mayo Sauce for Fish

In food processor combine a large sprig of dill, mayonnaise, and lemon. Set this sauce in the refrigerator until serving.

Button Down Collards

½ pound fresh collards
    or one box of
    frozen collard
    greens

A few dabs of butter
    and salt

If fresh collards are used, shred them. If frozen, thaw and boil until all ice is gone. Sauté the collards in butter for about 5 minutes. Season with salt. Serve lukewarm. Collards may not be available in your local market. Substitute canned carrots, but for this occasion make sure to buy Julienne carrots. It's a little more expensive, but after all, there are just so many subtle ways to say "I love you."

Columbia Law Tort

1 pound cake	1 bag of crushed
1 can of chocolate sauce	nuts

Slice the cake into ½-inch slices. Cover with the nuts and top with the chocolate sauce.

The Numbers Game

Winston Birge III, is coming to sup. He's bringing the other two-thirds—wife Binky and daughter Bunky. Their son Ned would have been a fourth, but he is doing his second, second semester at Bowdoin. Wee Bee Three, as his friends call him, never went to grad school because at his wedding at St. James' his bride Binky was well into her tenth week. But no matter, his second cousin at First Pennsylvania has steered him into ninth from the top. What to make for Wee Bee and the fractions? Try something from the Third World and, of course, have plenty of fifths of scotch.

Appetizers

Posh paté. See page 67 for posh paté

Main Course

Cashmere Curry with Pine Manor Nuts*
Minute Rice
American or English Court Squash

Dessert

Something in a bright pink—jello or
  sherbet

Cashmere Curry

4 or 5 chicken breasts
  peeled and
  boned
Oil to cover the bottom
  of the pan to
  about ½-inch deep
4 onions peeled and
  sliced
1 jar pine nuts
  (you can use
  almonds instead)

1 can prepared curry
  sauce (or 1 stick or
  bar of
  prepared curry
  paste and 1 cup of
  water,
  or 1 jigger
  cornstarch,
1 can chicken
  broth, curry
  powder, a little
  water)

Ask the butcher to skin, bone, and cube the
chicken. (Call him Sir.) Season with salt and
garlic. It is best to do this a day ahead. Brown the
chicken lightly in the oil and, without removing
it, pour out the remaining oil. (No, it does not
clog the drain.) Add the onions and:

The prepared curry sauce (or the stick or paste,
which you crumble, or the apple sauce, the curry powder, and the broth and water mixed with
the cornstarch). Cover the pot and cook for
about ½ hour. (Time for 2 straight scotches.) A
rule of thumb is that one whole breast will yield
enough chicken for 5/8 of a person.

Serve on a bed of rice and sprinkle on top with
the nuts.

Squash

1 small zucchini squash Very little water
  per person
Salt and pepper

Slice the squash into thin pieces, season, add water and simmer until soft. About five minutes. For English Court Squash, add more water, use no salt or pepper and cook for one hour.

If you are tired of chicken you can substitute shrimp (cleaned of course). If you prefer salad to squash, lettuce leaves with chick peas (drained of course) are nice, too.

Jello or Sherbet

Whether you use jello or sherbet, smother with coconut flakes and add lots of bourbon.

Gator Aid

Alligators are such dear little symbols for Ivy Leaguers that we are including a list of interesting recipes made with alligator meat. No crocodile tears now. You know we are just joshing.

1. Swamp bouillon
2. Alligator roast with Yorkshire Pudding.
3. Alligator tail ragout
4. Alligator balls en croute
5. Everglades stew*
6. Breast of alligator with preppy sauce
7. Peppered Izod
8. Alligator legs provençale
9. Alligator gumbo
10. Pressed alligator steaks (plain calf is used)
12. Gatorade
13. Alligator pears.

Everglades Stew

1 lb. alligator chuck	3 onions peeled and
6 Idaho potatoes	sliced

BREAST OF ALLIGATOR
(REMOVE LABEL BEFORE COOKING)

POACHED ALLIGATOR PEAR
(POIRE BELLE HELENE)

1 cup "tangy tomato
    sauce" (see page 67
    for recipe)

garlic powder, salt, and
    pepper

Have the game keeper or butcher cut the alligator chuck into cubes. (Call him Sir.) Discard all entrails (gruel), but save the skin for purses and belts. Season the meat thoroughly with the garlic, pepper and salt and brown at high temperature in the bottom of a pan. Add tomato sauce, a splash of water and the onions. Lower flame, cover and cook for about an hour. Peel and slice the potatoes into large cubes. Add to the stew and continue cooking until the potatoes are very soft. About ½ hour. (Time for 2 G and Ts.) If the sauce is too thick, add a liberal splash of water or red wine. Serves 3 or 4. (*Note*: Beef, veal, or lamb cubes may be substituted for alligator.)

Who's on First?

Of course, you know, one of the best hostesses in town is Taylor Ruth. Last month she had a party for Cabot John's engagement to Lindsay David. It was such fun. Cabot met Lindsay at the home of Winthrop Beverly. The person that actually introduced them was McArthur Stephen, and then Paley Robert invited them together to Robin Livingston's graduation party. Anyway, to get to the point, Taylor is a great cook. Sometimes the sequence of courses is a little whacky, but here's the menu at that wonderful party.

Appetizers

Fruit cocktail with lady fingers dipped in brandy

Main Course

Rah-Rah Avis (honeyed chicken)*
Mint Sherbet
Lime aspic (jello)

Dessert

Fitzgerald Mary's Bloody Gazpacho with cheese

Rah-Rah Avis

2 chickens cut into eighths (get some extra thighs and drumsticks for more than 6 people)

½ cup Madeira Wine—more or less
½ cup honey—more or less
1 can of tomato paste
Teriyaki sauce

One day ahead of time, combine wine, tomato sauce, honey and pour over chicken lightly seasoned with salt, garlic and pepper. Cover and refrigerate. On the day of the party, pick through the canned fruit cocktail for all the grapes you can find and set them aside. Roast the chicken at 375°, uncovered for about one hour. (Time for 2 vodkas and O.J.s.) Serve cool with the grapes, and the sherbet.

Bloody Gazpacho

To a generous amount of your Bloody Mary recipe (every Ivy Leaguer has one) add cucumbers, peppers and radishes that have been mushed up in the food processor. Top with croutons and ladle out from a punch bowl into mugs. Serve with crackers and Jarlsberg cheese.

(*Note*: The lime aspic can be prepared with sliced bananas or sliced cucumbers set into the jello. Both are great!)

Cooking Tongues

By now, we'd bet dollars to Burberry muffins that you love cooking, and occasionally while reading the marriage announcements, you glance at a recipe or two. That's fine. We know we're not the *dernier cri,* but a warning is due. Some of the terms you'll see are a mite confusing and can have other meanings. Here's a list of some "double entendre" cooking expressions.

1. Stewed, fried, potted, and boiled are not what you may think.
2. Neither is pickled
3. Pot
4. Fruitcake
5. Rump
6. Nutty
7. Dough
8. Bread
9. Browning
10. Rosemary
11. Pig out (this could be a Latin barbecue)
12. Sponge

MINCING

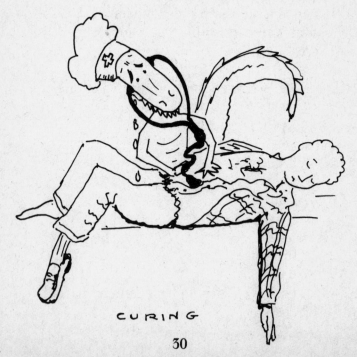

CURING

13. Tart
14. Breast
15. Prick
16. Balls
17. Faggot (in haute cuisine this means a few
    sprigs of parsley with celery and onion)
18. Chuck
19. Rich
20. Essence
21. Flaming
22. Cream
23. Take a leek
24. Curing
25. Mincing

FOR STEWED PREPPIE,
MARINATE WITH
RED WINE

SADDLE OF LAMB
(EASTERN STYLE)

Chic of Araby

Owen and Leslie Fletcher are the most darling couple. "Fletch" as he is called, and "Stretch" as she is called (she's 5'11") have lived in the Middle East. He works for an oil company and they both just gush with funny stories. They just had a baby named John, whose nickname is Juan (like in won-ton) because he was conceived in the airport in Spain during a two-hour layover from Riyadh. See what we mean? Many of their other stories are hilarious tales about trying to get hard liquor in Moslem countries. When they come for dinner serve something sort of oriental. What about lamb?

Appetizer

Wasp Nest Soup

Main Course

Saddle of Lamb Rosemary Hall*
Sourmash Potatoes
String beans on lettuce

Dessert

Vanilla Ice Cream with Southern Comfort

Wasp Nest Soup

1 abondoned wasp nest
1 Oriental style
   dehydrated
   soup mix with
   noodles

2 cans of celery juice
   or dehydrated leek
   soup (2 envelopes)
Water (only if leek soup
   is used)

Wash the wasp nest thoroughly (no detergents, just water). Marinate in equal mixtures of brandy and wine vinegar for about one week. On the day of serving, place the nest (without marinade) in the bottom of the pan. Add the celery juice or the leek soup mixed with about 3 cups of water. Simmer for about 20 minutes. Serve with soy sauce. Serves 4.

Saddle of Lamb

1 leg of lamb
About ½ cup of
   Teriyaki sauce
An equal amount of pre-
   pared mustard

Rosemary
Sliced onions

Have the lamb boned. Don't forget what you call the butcher. Marinate overnight with a mixture of the other ingredients. On the day of serving, place the lamb in a covered roasting pan. Pour the marinade and the onions over the lamb. Roast, covered for one hour. (Time for 2 martinis.) Remove cover and roast another 15 minutes. Remove the lamb and cut into thin slices. Return to the gravy and keep warm until serving. Serves 6.

Serve the lamb with a salad of lettuce leaves with cold string beans, sprinkled with a little vinegar, and sourmash potatoes.

Sourmash Potatoes

Peel and boil six Idaho potatoes. When soft, drain and mash with butter, milk, and a little Kentucky sour mash. Place in an oven-proof serving dish, and keep warm in the oven until serving time. The liquor is optional, but it can't hurt.

FROZEN ASSETS

More on Assets

Ivy Leaguers do have to evince an occasional interest in their investments. How else can we perpetuate the smooth-brow life? Get to know your investment counselor and invite him/her with some of your other fascinating friends. Make it buffet—"over the counter." The following are some high return ideas for things to serve:

1. Trussed account turkey
2. Mutual Fundue*
3. New York Pea Soup Stock (made with chicken bones)
4. American Onion Soup Stock (made with beef bones)
5. Jellied tomato bouillon (see page 67 for recipe)
6. Coin potatoes
7. Broiled stakes
8. Any of the futures items (corn, wheat, sugar, cocoa, soybean). Leave out pork bellies (gruel).
9. Apple computer compote

10. Fortune 500 cookies
11. Profiteroles
12. Frozen Assets

For an up evening serve the above with Dow Jones Punch and mixed drinks.

Dow Jones Punch

Strawberry sherbet	Champagne
Ginger ale	

Mix all three. Whenever the punch bowl is almost empty, pour in 3 glasses of champagne to one each of ginger ale and sherbet.

Mutual Fundue

3 cups of white wine	Lots of pepper
2 packages of Gruyere cheese triangles	2 teaspoons or about
Any left over Jarlsberg	1 Jigger of cornstarch

Grate the cheese in the food processor (can be done days ahead of time). Use a casserole dish over an alcohol burner. If you don't have one, ask any of your parents' friends who were married in the 1950s. Otherwise, improvise. Warm about one-half of the wine, but do not boil. Add one-half of the cheese. When it gets creamy, add half of the cornstarch, and add pepper. Reserve the remaining wine, cheese and cornstarch to keep adding as the party progresses. Serve chunks of slightly stale french bread for dipping into the bubbling mixture. Serves 10.

Roman Holiday

Freddy Smith Paxton is engaged! Everyone is talking about it. Freddy, whose real name is Frederica, is a bona fide preppie. She went to Chapin until 8th grade. Then she went on to Miss Porter's. From there she went to Sweet Briar, spent her junior year in Paris, graduated with a 2.5 G.P.A. and interned at Sotheby's for a year. She came out at the Plaza, the St. Regis, and it's rumored she was seen at the Holiday Inn right next to the Holland Tunnel one of those nights. Her fiancé is named Roger Pizzaroni. He went to Public School 66 in the Bronx, then to Junior High School 98, and for two years to James Monroe High School, also in the Bronx. They say he may go back to school now that he's in love. Freddy won't say just how she met Roger. You can bet her parents are in a snit about it, but what can they do? Freddy is such a terrific friend, she derserves a party in her honor. Here are a few suggestions: Remember it's good form to make Roger feel at home.

Appetizers

Tiny pizzas

ALs

AL FRESCO   AL DENTE

HERBS

HERBERT A.   HERBERT
TROPHY, III   BARR NUNN JR.

40

Manicotti (see page 67 for recipe for "Marvelous Manicotti")

Main Course

Al Dente's Marinara Sauce with Meat*
Green salad

Dessert

Coffee ice cream with cookies

Al Dente's Marinara Sauce with Meat

1 lb. ground chuck or round steak	Olive oil
2 medium-size cans of crushed tomatoes	Garlic and salt to taste
1 small can tomato paste	

Heat the oil to cover the bottom of the pan to a depth of about ½ inch. Add the crushed tomatoes, including the canned liquids. Sprinkle with salt, and add the ground meat, breaking up the chunks into the sauce. Add lots of garlic and simmer, uncovered for about one hour. (Time for 3–4 glasses of red wine.) Then, add the tomato paste, mix, and just before serving douse the whole mixture with red wine. This delicious sauce should be served with linguini or spaghetti and grated cheese. Serves 4–6.

Green Salad

A green salad should have lettuce, cucumbers, water cress, and endive if you feel like it. See page 67 for "Great Italian Salad Dressing."

HOME FRIES

Meals on Wheels

Everyone loves a picnic and Ivy Leaguers are no exception. Just about anything you eat "Al Fresco" is delicious, but here are some ideas that will make your picnic original and outrageous.

1. Virginia Mayos—Decrusted white bread with the thinnest slices of Virginia ham, and just a smidge of mayo. Divine with beer.
2. Fried chicken—Available at many franchises. Great with Bloodys.
3. Cream cheese and jam sandwiches—Intense with sours.
4. Pickled pickles—Cucumbers marinated in rye. Great with ginger ale.
5. Hard-boiled eggs—Original, and super with bourbon.
6. American cheese on white—Awesome with mustard and gin and tonic.
7. Leftover turkey, ham, roast beef or meat loaf—Fabulous with wine.

8. Cream cheese and watercress mix—Everyone makes their own sandwiches. To die from with vodka.

If a grill is available, the following will just blow you away.

1. Hot dogs (non-kosher please!)
2. Ribs marinated in barbecue sauce mixed with gin.
3. Tartan skirt steaks*
4. Marshmallows—Toasted while more drinks are passed.
5. Home fries—Yummers with everything.

Tartan Skirt Steaks

Skirt steaks (tenderloin)   Teriyaki sauce
   1 to a person   Scotch
Sweet and sour sauce—see
   page 67 for recipe

Spread steaks in one layer. Coat with a mixture of sweet and sour sauce, scotch, and teriyaki sauce. Leave for about one hour or longer. (Time for 3 beers.) Grill quickly on both sides over flaming coals.

Getting On

When Ivy Leaguers are in their fifties they develop a leathery patina. They are usually successful. Their children are now grown Ivy Leaguers with their own membership in the nice clubs. They still have many of the same friends they had in their teens. Getting together with them is still fun and the menus have barely changed. Sometimes, however, the following happens on the day before a dinner party.

Skip Worthington calls to say that she and Biff will be happy to come tomorrow, but she thought she should mention that Biff has just developed diabetes, so he can't have carbohydrates at all. That means no bread, no rice, no dessert and, worst of all, no drinks.

The phone is barely on the cradle when Alison Beardsley calls to say how she's looking forward to tomorrow, but Ford just got back from the doctor's office, and his pressure is too high and he simply must avoid all salt and lose ten pounds. So, she just thought she'd mention it in case it interfered with your plans in any way.

You guessed it, the third couple also has a problem. Jack and Cookie Butterworth just took a liver test and scored very high grades. Don't congratulate them! That means trouble and no drinking—not even wine! They'd like to come, but it would be an ordeal watching the others drink, so please forgive.

What to do about tomorrow's dinner party and all those finicky eaters? See page 67 for a suggestion.

Pillow Talk

A Sleepover! What fun! If it's at your house, remember the way to the heart, anatomically as well as symbolically, is through the stomach. You prepare the breakfast the morning after. Naturally, include drinks, but be forewarned. As the Bard put it: "It provoketh the desire, but diminisheth from the act..." Here are some breakfast suggestions:

Eyeopener Orange Juice—½ champagne, ½ o.j.
Eggs Up Andover*
White bread, toasted, with orange marmalade
Strawberries and bananas
Suggest, but don't insist on bran
Coffee or tea with a tiny splash of sherry

Eggs Up Andover

2 eggs per person   Salt and pepper
1 dab butter

Put a dab of butter in the bottom of a frying pan. Just when it sizzles add two eggs. Please try to

EGGS UP ANDOVER

do this without messing up the yolk. When the white part hardens a bit, ever so gently try to turn the eggs over without making the yolk run. *If* the yolk is broken either in the beginning or when you are trying to turn the eggs, immediately scramble the eggs with a fork, and pretend that's how you meant to do them all along. Sprinkle with salt and pepper. *Don't* allow the eggs to cool too much. Try to practice this dish in your own home until you get it right. And remember, runny whites are gruel.

MiXiNG

J.L.T.
(Just Like That)

How about a party? Think of a reason. That shouldn't be hard for you—a new job, a new lease, good grades, failing grades, a new heart-throb—anything at all can be a good excuse for a party. Make it memorable for everyone, including yourself. We'll show you how to do it the easy way. Invite anyone you feel like, and even throw in a few non-Ivy League types. Who says a dentist or an actuary can't be fun? First of all, prepare the bar as follows:

Several jugs of white and red wine. If you are expecting a big crowd, use plastic glasses, but only get one size, shaped like small tumblers. (Plastic glasses with stems tip over too easily.) Get rye, bourbon, scotch, vodka, gin, and brandy. Beer, too. For mixers prepare O.J., ginger ale, club soda, water, tomato juice, cranberry juice cocktail, vermouth, and tonic. Have tabasco, Worcestershire sauce, limes, olives, capers, bitters, pearl onions, and lemon. How much? That's easy too.

Drink Chart

Very Approximate

No. of Guests	Total No. of Drinks	No. of 750 ml bottles	No. of litre bottles
4	16	1	¾
6	24	a few	a few
8	32	several	several
10	40	many	many
12	48	plenty	plenty

For more than 12, multiply by pie-eyed[2] × the number of guests and just get cases. Remember the stuff ages well, and you are going to have more parties.

Now for the food part:

Peanuts, potato chips, pretzels, cheese doodles

Rabbit food: celery, carrots, cucumbers, zucchini with a clam dip (see page 67 for "perfect clam dip")

Marinated mushrooms—any store-bought variety

Jarlsberg cheese and triscuits

Black olives

Bread sticks

Antipasto plate—hard salami, more olives, more celery, ham and cheese slices rolled together

Liverwurst—served in a mug with crackers

That should satisfy just about everyone. Now, almost as important as the drinks are the ice cubes. Have plenty. Keep making cubes a few days ahead of time and keep them in plastic bags in the freezer. If they seem to have frozen together whack the bag with a hammer a few times. Ice cubes should be large, dry, and frosty so that they don't dilute the drinks.

These are the makings of a perfect party, but remember, the party is only as good as the host. Be friendly, laid back, and cheerful. Also, allow your guests to fend for themselves. Just sort of wave in the direction of the drinks and food. If they're worth inviting, they'll do the rest. Have a blast.

L.L. BEANS
YES!

DESIGNER
BEANS
NO!

Big Leaguers

Every so often it's fun to have a brunch, or a luncheon, or a big evening supper party just to celebrate being an Ivy Leaguer. Sure, other people can also be fun, but it really is so special just being you. How to put it? Well, ethnic is in, so we won't beat about the bush...We're beautiful! For a party like this every single dish should have a symbolic meaning, so here are some perfect suggestions:

1. Regatta rice—see page 67
2. L.L. bean soup*
3. Broccoli au Groton*
4. Racquet of lamb*
5. Beef Madeira*
6. Brooks Brothers trout*
7. Squash
8. Club steaks*
9. Pearl onions
10. Concord grapes
11. Deerfield venison
12. Bermuda Shop onions

STUFFED BASS WITH
BROCOLI GROTON

13. Deck ducks*
14. Harvard beets
15. Boston lettuce
16. Preppy punch*
17. Stuffed bass
18. Preppy pork*
19. Boola Boola soup

L.L. Bean Soup

Brown 2 strips of bacon until it gets crisp. Add chopped onions (2). 1 can of cream of tomato soup and 1 can of baked beans and about ½ can of water. Simmer and serve. Yummy!

Broccoli au Groton

1 pk. frozen broccoli   ½ cup milk
     spears
½ cup Cheeze-Whiz
     processed cheese
     spread

Prepare broccoli according to directions. Top with a sauce made of cheese spread and the milk. Heat until the cheese bubbles.

Racquet of Lamb

1 crown roast of lamb
     seasoned with salt,
     pepper, oil and a dab of
     Dijon mustard.

Have the butcher prepare the lamb in the form of a crown. (Remember to call him Sir.) Roast at 325° for about 1½ hours. Fill the center with regatta rice mixed with green peas. Divine!

BOOLA BOOLA SOUP
(SERVED IN YALE BOWL)

Beef Madeira

1½ lbs. beef chuck
   cut into cubes
1½ cups Madeira wine

Salt and pepper
and garlic powder

Season the meat heavily and marinate in the wine overnight. Remove from the marinade and brown, then add the marinade. Cover and cook for about 2 hours. Serve with noodles.

Brooks Brothers Trout

Ask the fishman to remove the fins, but leave the heads and tails. Dip in milk and roll in flour mixed with salt and pepper. Fry in hot oil, and keep warm until serving. Great with cole slaw.

Club Steaks

Any economy steaks such as fillet, chuck, round, marinated in tenderizer and wine for about a day. Grilled or broiled, they are just right with canned veggies and a pretty salad.

Deck Ducks

Cook ducks like goose, for a long time. Prick often. Make a super sauce as follows: Combine 1 cup sugar, 1 cup o.j., a jigger of orange marmalade, and a jigger of cornstarch. Boil over a medium flame until it starts to thicken. Add liqueur and serve over crisp duck.

Ivy League Pork

Buy a rolled pork roast. Season thoroughly with teriyaki sauce, garlic, salt, and pepper. Roast at 350° for 2 hours. Serve with sauerkraut.

All the above recipes can be served with a whole variety of vegetables. Squash is great. Lima beans are superb. Harvard beets are so appropriate. String beans, carrots, and spinach are lovely. For starches use potatoes, rice, noodles, in just about any style.

For desserts, we recommend lady fingers, oreo cookies, sherbets, and jellos. Make sure that the jello and sherbet is in one of the Lily Pulitzer colors.

Wines and liquors should always be plentiful, and the following punch is nice too.

Ivy League Punch

Sliced oranges and strawberries swimming around in a mixture of champagne and white wine. Any proportions you want.

Co-Eat-Us

Somehow, we feel that we've really given you some great ideas for just about every occasion, except for theme parties. Our favorite theme party is a big, licentious, loud, orgy. And here are some menu suggestions for all types of taste.

1. Rump steak
2. Cocktails (natch)
3. Breast of anything
4. Anything served on a bed of something
5. Nectar punch
6. "Are You Game Hen?"
7. Chicken
8. Parsley and mints (for breath)
9. Capers
10. Tenderizer
11. Saucy sauces
12. Tarts
13. Rolls
14. Loins of anything
15. Picadillo
16. Whore's d'oeuvres
17. Flageolets (very kinky)

COOLING YOUR BUNS

COCKALEEKIE
SOUP

18. Skinny dip
19. Nuts
20. Coq au vin
21. Mixed fry
22. Sauce Bordelloaise
23. Caviar Emptor
24. Afro-dizzy-ak (see page 67)

TENDERIZE

The Forgettable Meal

Ivy Leaguers occasionally have conflicts. Mummy's charity committee wants to meet for lunch *chez vous*. It's not proper form to refuse, but here's a menu that will virtually guarantee that you won't be asked to cook for the girls again. Remember, that it's style over taste, so serve the following with the same pleasant servility that one expects from a colleen at Schrafft's.

Drinks

Offer a choice of Bloodys, G&T, chilled white wine, and anything straight. (No beer for this one please!)

Appetizers

Canned shrimp (undrained) & fishsticks (shortcook them so they remain ice cold in the center)

Main Course

Ham steaks with canned pineapple rings.
No seasoning. Brown only slightly.

Side Dish

(Please follow directions carefully)

1 lb. #8 spaghetti (or
macaroni)
Lots of water (about 2
quarts)

No salt
1 lb. Cheddar cheese or
American cheese

Boil spaghetti (or macaroni) until all the water
is gone. Be sure not to burn. Add the cheese and
toss. Put in a baking dish and warm at 300° or so
until the cheese is totally melted. Serves 6–8.
Can be made hours ahead of time.

Place the "pasta" and the ham on individual
plates. Serve a side salad of lettuce leaves with
canned string beans.

Dessert

Jello (any flavor)
Oreo cookies
Coffee or tea

Gourmet Guide

Nitty gritty	Pre-cooked instant cous-cous
Perfect mayonnaise	Miracle Whip
Perfect salad dressing	Miracle Whip
Heavenly dip	Philadelphia brand onion dip
Post paté	Spam
Tangy tomato sauce	Hunt's
Jellied tomato bouillon	Cross & Blackwell
Marvelous manicotti	Frozen Franco-American
Great Italian salad dressing	Wishbone
Sweet and sour sauce	Save from Chinese take-out
Finicky eaters	Cancel party
Perfect clam dip	Philadelphia brand clam dip
Regatta rice	Minute rice
Afro-dizzy-ak	Black rum straight

Extra Credits (Point 1)

In spite of the sad lack of space, we simply cannot ignore some celebrated dishes that are served at those gourmets' paradises, the Ivy League college dining halls, and sometimes even spooned up by the cook at home.

A mouth-watering sampling follows, cunningly conjured up in picture form, after all a picture is worth 10,000 words and who wants to read 10,000 words?

HOLY MACKEREL
A LA GRECQUE

ARROZ CON POLO

SCALLOPPED
POTATOES

MOOSE AU CHOCOLAT

MACKINTOSH APPLE TART
(BELT CASUALLY BUCKLED IN BACK)

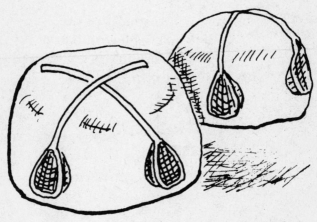

HOT LA CROSSE BUNS

Extra Credits (Point 2)

For those of you still a smidge unsure of certain odd-sounding cooking instructions, these handy household hints are in picture form (so much easier on the eyes)!

ON SHORT NOTICE, PREPPIES
WILL EVEN CATER AN AFFAIR.

PREPPING YOUR PREP
(TRUSSING)

WHIPPING

STUFFING

FOLDING AND CUTTING

SALT AND PEPPER SLACKS
(WATCH YOUR TAIL ...)

DUSTING
ON
POWDERED
SUGAR IS
A PIECE OF
CAKE....

Finis

Well, we've just gone to the absolute max with recipes and suggestions. If you add, delete, and substitute ingredients creatively, you are ready to cope with any event. In fact, you may never need another cookbook, unless you need more ideas for mixing drinks. If that's the case, just ask a fellow Ivy Leaguer. If you do trip upon a cookbook with a promising title—one with words like "half-hour, instant, easy, no care," etc.—look it over. However, remember that many boresville classics turn up in paperbacks with lurid, suggestive covers. When you read cooking instructions always ask yourself the following questions:

1. "Is it truly top drawer second rate?"
2. "Can I serve it lukewarm?"
3. "Can I do this while high?"
4. "Can I do this while drunk?"
5. "Can I clean up afterward even while extremely intoxicated?"
6. "If I overcook this is it still edible?"

7. "Can Broccoli, brussel sprouts, and cauliflower truly taste identical?"
8. "Does it omit all gruel?"
9. "Can I add more liquor?"
10. "Does it rank high on the GRE (get ready earlier)?"

The answers must be positive. Otherwise scratch it—too heavy duty. It is definitely rude city not to drink with your guests.

The last bit of advice is not to try for the memorable. In fact, by the time cordials are served, the meal should have receded into forgetfulness. And, if your party is truly a good one, by the next morning your guests should be unable to even think of food.

Hey! Good luck!